Hooray! I'm Catholic!

Written by Hana Cole

Illustrated by Joanna Steege

Ambassador
Children's Books
Mahwah • New Jersey

Library of Congress Cataloging-in-Publication Data

Cole, Hana, 1953-
  Hooray! I'm Catholic! / written by Hana Cole ; illustrated by Joanna Steege.
     p. cm.
  ISBN 978-0-8091-6746-3 (alk. paper)
  1. Catholic Church--Juvenile literature. I. Steege, Joanna. II. Title.
  BX948.C65 2010
  282--dc22
                              2009050476

Published by Ambassador Books
An imprint of Paulist Press
997 Macarthur Boulevard
Mahwah, New Jersey 07430

www.ambassadorbooks.com

Printed and bound in the United States
By Versa Press, East Peoria, IL
September 2014

Hooray for Michael and Daniel!
Hooray! Hooray! Hooray!

— H.C.

For my parents, who taught me to go live
the life I have imagined.

— J.S.

What makes being Catholic great?
Lots of little things—
candles, bells, and blessings,
feathery angel wings,

stained glass every morning,
rosaries to hold tight,
vestments changing through the year—
purple, green, or white.

What makes being Catholic great?
Lots of big things, too!
Knowing Jesus loves me,
knowing he loves you,

knowing that forever—
forever and a day—
Jesus holds me by the hand,
showing me the way.

What makes being Catholic great?
Lots of little things—

Baby Jesus smiling,
camels, gifts, and kings,

angels high in heaven,
single star so bright,
Mary at her baby's side,
watching through the night.

What makes being Catholic great?
Lots of big things too!
Jesus in Communion,
close to me and you,

Good News from the Bible,
blessings we receive,
side by side and hand in hand,
saying, "We believe!"

What makes being Catholic great?
Lots of little things—
ashes on my forehead,

palms like angel wings,

kneeling at each Station
around the church's wall,

bunnies, lilies, butterflies—
chocolate eggs for all!

What makes being Catholic great?
Lots of big things too!
Jesus died to save us.
That means me and you.

All alone and frightened,
we had lost our way.
Jesus brought us home again,
and now we're here to stay.

What makes being Catholic great?
I do! So do you!
Lots of ways of helping
that even kids can do:
tulips for Miss Reyes,

milk for Mr. Ko,

dogs to wash and dogs to walk,
shovels full of snow.

Twenty-seven pairs of socks!

Lacy hearts of red,

dollars for the missions,

bowls of soup with bread.

Praying for the homeless,
praying for the poor,
praying for the moms and dads
and children hurt by war.

What makes being Catholic great?
Jesus knows my name,
knows my heart's a candle—
tiny glowing flame.

Church brings us together,
and there my little light
can join with yours to show the world
that heaven's shiny bright.

Hooray! Hooray!
I'm Catholic!
I'm Catholic every day!
Jesus loves us—me and you.
Hooray! Hooray! Hooray!

About the Author

Hana Cole was the pen name of Susan Heyboer O'Keefe. For over twenty years, she wrote and published many books for children, including quite a few on Christian and Catholic spirituality, and was a frequent and popular presenter at writers' conferences and workshops. A life-long resident of New Jersey, Susan passed away in December 2013, but she lives on in her books.

About the Illustrator

Joanna Steege is a graduate of Savannah College of Art and Design. She was born in Atlanta, Georgia, where she lives and works. This is her first children's book.

Ambassador
Children's Books
Mahwah • New Jersey